Handknitting with Meg Swansen

Handknitting

with

Meg Swansen

Schoolhouse Press

Photographs and drawings: Schoolhouse Press

© 1995 Meg Swansen

Schoolhouse Press
6899 Cary Bluff
Pittsville, WI 54466

Second Printing May '96
Printed in the United States of America

ISBN 0-942018-08-7

preface

Meg Swansen and her mother Elizabeth Zimmermann comprised a knitting team for many decades. They wrote magazine articles as well as their semi-annual publication Wool Gathering, ran a mail-order knitting-supply business, published books, held their annual Knitting Camp conventions and together with Meg's composer/videographer husband Chris, they produced instructional handknitting videos. Elizabeth retired in 1990 and Meg and Chris continue with all the above activities.

This book is a compilation of Meg's designs from Wool Gathering issues #42 through #48. Although there is sufficient information in the printed instructions, an accompanying video which shows the garment being knitted from casting-on to casting-off has proven helpful to scores of knitters. Seeing SSK, or Applied I-Cord being worked makes it generally easier to assimilate; after all, being shown a new skill or technique pre-dates the printed word.

Schoolhouse Press, started by Elizabeth in 1959, has grown to become a complete mail-order source for all knitter's needs - as well as a publisher of handknitting books and videos. A separate video is available to accompany each chapter in this book and we will be pleased to send a catalogue upon request.

Schoolhouse Press
6899 Cary Bluff
Pittsville, WI 54466
September, 1995

Introduction

When thoughts turn to the triumphs of knitters of ages past we cannot help but wonder how much knitting knowledge has been lost. Regrettably, today's knitting often confirms the narrowness of our conceptual boundaries. Meg Swansen, however, not only turns the tide of lost knowledge but makes bold dashes to the frontier, time after time.

Handknitting with Meg Swansen is not a book that will be forgotten in a year or two. The presence of her mother/mentor Elizabeth Zimmermann hovers lightly over its pages and homage is paid to the late and great of the knitting world, but this book is unmistakably *Meg*. Her ideas, her methods, and her strong sense of classic style continue to flourish - and to nourish. We are thankful for it.

Few knitters have Meg's remarkable intuition about knitted forms. Whether it's creeping up the sides of a parallelogram to change the grain of the fabric or building gloves from the fingertips to the wrist she frequently breaks the barriers of accepted practice. Her emphasis on achieving perfect fit *by careful knitting alone* has become a Swansen signature.

This book is both challenging and deeply refreshing. Using the highly effective project method of instruction, Meg teaches skills that will enrich our knitting lives for years to come. Sharp bits of innovation cosy up against familiar techniques that we have come to know and love. Old favourites like the Phoney Seam and the Sewn Casting Off make cameo appearances while trail blazers like Jogless

Colour-Pattern Knitting are introduced in careful detail. In a field where non-standard technical terminology often muddies the waters, Meg deserves showers of praise for her crystal clear explanations. Diagrams and photographs are generously used and supply important mind maps for more complicated manoeuvres.

There is charm and humour here too. Feline stars of stage and screen add grace to the pages, and the use of "real people" models, many of whom are familiar to us, strengthens our sense of community. Meg's own persuasive way with words encourages the most doubtful knitters to stretch a little. Lace knitting, for example, is no more difficult than making a soufflé, she insists. "It's mostly air and really no trick at all!"

And so Meg Swansen pilots willing knitters to adventure and to excellence once again. Advanced knitters will be exhilarated and novice knitters will sprout wings!

Shirley Scott
August, '95
Author of *Canada Knits;*
a.k.a. "Shirl the Purl" founder of *Knitters News,*
the Canadian Hand Knitting Newsletter

Knitting books from Schoolhouse Press

Knitting Workshop, Elizabeth Zimmermann

Knitting Around, Elizabeth Zimmermann

Barbara Abbey's Knitting Lace

Notes on Double Knitting, Beverly Royce

Designs for Knitting Kilt Hose & Knickerbocker Stockings, Veronica Gainford

Handknitting with Meg Swansen

Knitting series from Schoolhouse Video

Knitting Workshop, Elizabeth Zimmermann

Knitting Glossary, Elizabeth Zimmermann and Meg Swansen

Knitting Around, Elizabeth Zimmermann and Meg Swansen

Handknitting with Meg Swansen

Handknitting with Meg Swansen

Chapter

CHAPTER ONE

Puzzle-Pillow Blanket

September 1991. Dear Knitter,

The Puzzle-Pillow offers knitting satisfaction on many levels: it is an intriguing concept to grasp initially; quite simple to execute, yet incorporates several challenging options. The finished item exudes an aura of mystery (our fave), and even our son, Cully - Mr Physics - was hard put to re-assemble the pillow from the spread out blanket.

We first came upon this concept (originator sought, but not found) in the form of a Quilt Pillow which we thought was simply a pillow cover. However, when we reached into the quilted cover and pulled out an *attached* blanket, we were startled! Naturally, our thoughts turned to a knitted version, and we came up with the following design.

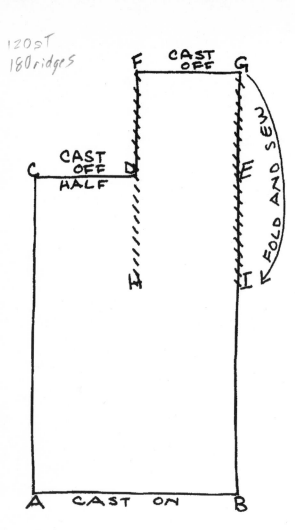

120 st
180 ridges

F CAST OFF G

C CAST OFF HALF D

FOLD AND SEW

E

H

I

A CAST ON B

Hesitant knitters may simply cast on across the lower edge, knit to wanted height, cast off half the stitches, knit the pillow cover on the second half, fold it over and sew it down. You may wallow in lovely, uninterrupted Garter-Stitch, and perfect your knitting technique. Instructions and schematic for the basic shape are given here.

Simple PUZZLE-PILLOW For New or Un-sure Knitters

NOTE: 2 rows = 1 ridge.
SIZE: 24"x36" (28" x 42", 36"x54") Small (medium, large)
GAUGE: 3 stitches to 1"
MATERIALS: 20oz (28oz, 44oz) of 3-ply *Sheepswool* (or something to give you the wanted Gauge). A 24" circular needle (or a pair of s.p. needles) of a size to give you the required Gauge; approximately #9-11.

Refer to the drawing shown here, and ...

Cast On at *A-B* 72 (84, 108) stitches. Work back and forth in Garter-Stitch throughout. Knit straight to *C-D-E,*.. a total of 108 (126, 162) ridges (which is 216, 252, 324 rows). At *C-D* cast off 36 (42, 54) stitches. Knit on remaining 36 (42, 54) stitches from *D-E* for 36 (42, 54) ridges. Cast off from *F* to *G*. Fold pillow flap *F-G* to *H-I*. Sew *F-D* to *D-H* and *G-E* to *E-I*. Done. *(to fold it into its pillow cover, see pp10,11))*

MORE CHALLENGING ZIG-ZAG PUZZLE - PILLOW

For a handsome braided selvedge, you may slip each first stitch Purlwise with wool in front, except when you are joining in a new color, at which time you will KNIT the first stitch. When the instructions say K22, it means Slip 1 P'wise, K21.

NOTE: 2 rows = 1 ridge.

SIZE: 24"x 36" (28"x 42", 36"x 54") Small (medium, large)

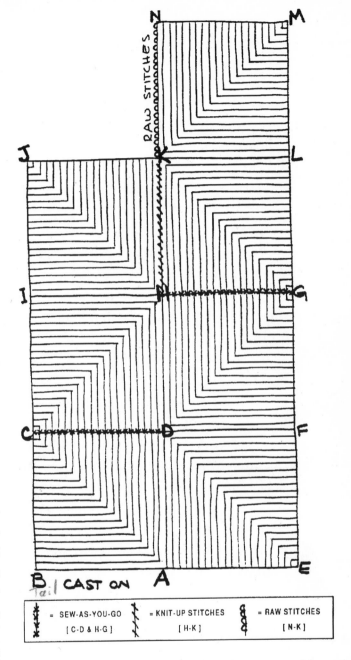

= SEW-AS-YOU-GO [C-D & H-G]	= KNIT-UP STITCHES [H-K]	= RAW STITCHES [N-K]

GAUGE: 3 stitches to 1"

MATERIALS: 3 (4, 6) 4oz skeins *each* of Main Color (MC) *and* contrasting color (CC) of 3-ply Sheepswool (or a wool to give you the needed Gauge). A 24" circular needle (or a pair of s.p. needles) of a size to give you the required Gauge; approximately #9-11. Two spare needles of the same size for the *"Sew" As You Go* and the *3-Needle I-Cord Cast Off* portions.

MC will always knit *triangles* with horizontal grain, CC will always knit *parallelograms* with vertical grain. Nice, huh? We didn't notice that until half way through the prototype ... so even if you knit this all in one color, the change of grain will highlight the zig-zag pattern. Refer to the drawing on page 5.

K 1st st after castonWith MC at *A-B*, **Cast On** 36 (42, 54). **Turn corner.** K35 (41, 53) ... yes, just leave the last stitch on the needle un-worked. Turn. and K 35 (41, 53) back (remembering to slip 1st stitch P'wise).

K34 (40, 52). Turn. Knit back.

K33 (39, 51). Turn. Knit back.

K32 (38, 50). Turn, Knit back, etc - abandoning one stitch at the same end (*A*) every other row, and slipping all first stitches as if to Purl.

Continue thus down to K2. Turn. Knit back. sl, K

NOW - Slip 1 p'wise. wrap 2ndTurn. Knit 1 stitch. Yes, quite reedickledockle (as *Pogo* says), but this assures a nice sharp corner. You are at *C*.

Break MC and join in CC.

K2 (actually knitting the first stitch just this one time). Turn. Knit back.

K3. Turn. Knit back.

K4. Turn, Knit back. etc, back up to ...

K36 (42, 54). Turn. Knit back. You are at the *A* end of *D-A*. K 5 3

... pay attention ...

You will immediately begin turning the 2nd side of the parallelogram, which causes you to abandon stitches on the opposite end of the needle (D) as follows:

K35 (41, 53). Turn. Knit back.

K34 (40, 52). Turn. Knit back., etc, down to Slip 1. Turn. Knit 1 at E.

Change to MC and

K2. Turn. Knit back.

K3. Turn. Knit back., etc, up to you full complement of stitches. You are now at *D-F* and this is one of only 3 times during the whole blanket where you will knit one full ridge (2 rows) on all stitches before leaving orphan stitches as you head for *G.* (This will happen again at *I-H* and at *K-L*).

At *G*, change back to CC and begin your second parallelogram, following the drawing on page 5.

At *H-D* you will start to leave stitches on the opposite end of the needle (as before) and At The Same Time, you may "Sew" As You Go if you like:

With one of the spare needles, beginning at the outside corner (*C*), pick up one stitch for each ridge along the selvedge *C-D* from the outline stitch furthest from you *(photo at right)*. You will find only 35 (41, 53) stitches because you began the CC with "K2", so pick up an additional thread and twist it into a stitch at *C*.

*Work to within last stitch at *D*, SSK *(see p81)* being last stitch on the needle, plus one picked-up stitch. Turn, slip 1 P'wise and work back to one stitch less at **H**. Repeat from * along **D-C** selvedge down to one stitch at **C**. Change to MC, and follow the drawing to **J**. Change to CC and follow to **K-H**.

Now, how fussy are you? Look at the **C-D** selvedge. See how different it is on each side of the blan? Do you want each of the two "Sew"-As-You-Go sections to match on each side? If you answer NO, then just repeat what you did the first time. If you answered YES, then **Pay Attention Again:**

With pick-up needle, beginning at outside corner **G**, pick up each selvedge stitch from the side closest to you. **Work to within last stitch at **H**, wool forward, Slip 2 P'wise (being last stitch plus one picked-up stitch). Turn, K2 together. Repeat from ** along **H-G** to one stitch. Change to MC and knit the final big triangle to **M**. Change to CC and work to **N-K**. **Do not cast off**, but leave the raw stitches on the needle.

With a spare needle and a new strand of CC, beginning at **H**, *Knit*-Up stitches as follows: find the ridge that links K to H. Insert the tip of the needle through one of the purl bumps of the ridge; hook the

working wool through. (*See photo at left*) Knit up stitch for stitch along **H-K**. Break wool. Fold **N-M** over to meet **H-G** and unite the pillow cover by working ... **3-Needle 2-stitch I-Cord Cast Off** as follows:

At **K**, with CC, Cast On 2 stitches onto your third needle. Holding the **raw-stitches needle** and the **knit-up needle** parallel to each other, transfer the two Cord stitches to the back needle. *K1, slip 1, K2 together (being one stitch each from front & back needles), psso. Replace

2 Cord stitches on back needle *(shown in photo below)*, and repeat from * across all stitches to **N/H** - which are now united. Both spare needles are free. Turn a corner by working a free row (roundlet) of the 2 Cord stitches without attaching them to anything.

Knit Elizabeth's **Applied I-Cord** across the pouch opening as follows: with spare needle, pick up 1 stitch for each ridge along **N-M** selvedge. *K 1 Cord stitch, K2 tog through-back-loops (being the second Cord stitch and one picked-up stitch). Replace the 2 Cord stitches to L needle, and repeat from * across **N-M.** Turn I-Cord corner in CC as before.

Now, pick up 1 stitch for each ridge along **M-L** and **L-G.** Join in MC and work 3-Needle 2-Stitch I-Cord Cast Off to unite **M-L** and **G-L.** Break wool. Finish off.

Because this blanket is totally reversible, it is worth it to take the time to splice in each new skein of wool as follows: separate 4" of the old wool end into its three component plies. Break off 3" of one strand and 2" of the second. Repeat on the new end, Overlap the ends, "moisten" (spit on) one palm and rub the two ends together to fuse the wool. Knit on. (If you find the spit part revolting, keep a dampened sponge next to your knitting chair.)

How to fold the blan into its pillow cover

1. Fold in half with the pillow cover on top

2. From inside pillow cover, grab free outside corner.

3. Fold pillow cover inside-out over top of blan.

4. Fold up bottom third

5. Tuck 4 folded thick-
nesses into pillow cover

6. Voilà. Thick, soft
pillow is born.

For your next Puzzle-Pillow, try knitting each
section in a different color for a Patchwork - changing
colors only at the corners to maintain total reversibility.
Try adding an I-Cord carrying strap for ease in
schlepping your pillow to football games, picnics,
kindergarten (for naps) or long car trips.

When snuggling down onto the sofa, we flip the
unfolded blanket over our legs with the pillow case
underneath and at the bottom; it makes a great Foot
Cozy.

CHAPTER TWO

Swedish Dubbelmössa and Scarf

March, 1991. Dear Knitter,

We are nothing if not responsive to our dear cussies, and there have been several requests recently for simpler designs. Here, then, is a project which is simplicity itself. Its evolution began with a 6-foot scarf Elizabeth had knitted for Gaffer in the 1950s: a Rugby Scarf. The magazine to whom she submitted it had fun pouring one of the models into it *(see photo)*. As you can imagine, this version causes you to cast on the circumference you want, and knit forever; putting in stripes now and then to prove that you are making headway. The open ends are hemmed. Upon its return from NY (along with the photos) Gaffer's attitude toward his scarf was forever altered.

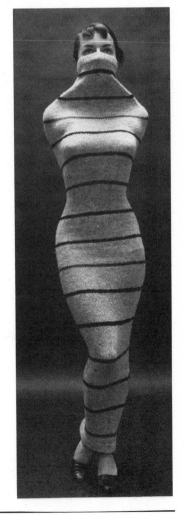

The next version was knitted a few years later, in much lighter-weight wool, with its ends closed in by knitting a gigantic sock toe fore and aft. This we realized, could double as a combination scarf **and** a hat by punching in one end, pulling it onto your head, and wrapping the tail around your neck. Aha! a Scat (or, I suppose, a Harf). On page 12, I am holding an old photo *(by Tom Zimmermann)* of that version from 1963.

When the outstanding Swedish knitting book *Binge* fell into our hands in 1981 (alas, now out-of-print), we immediately recognized the *Dubbelmössa,* and were delighted to learn that Elizabeth's "original" 1963 version used the same principle as a traditional Swedish stocking cap - not just punched in at one end, but punched in double, and folded up to produce a quadruple thickness about the ears and forehead. Lovely. Another example of Knitting Telepathy.

The "Scat" consists of a head-sized tube, the length of which is entirely up to you ... anything from a super long scarf to a shortish Very Warm Hat *(pp 42-43 of Knitting Around; see bibliography).* Onto this basic form you may add what you like in the way of color patterns. Should you decide to close off the two ends with a giant sock toe ... think of it ... the tube will be hermetically sealed. Yes! the "1-inch-carry" rule is out the window, and you may insert some of those forbidden color patterns which cause you to carry the second color 12-15 stitches across the back; no need to worry about fingers or buttons catching the long loops ... you need not twist the two colors around each other to span the distance.

If color pattern knitting is new to you, do not be fussed by the Jogless business at the end of the *Dubbelmössa* instructions. Just concentrate on your method of carrying the colors loosely across the back of the work. If you hold one color in each hand (or both in your left hand as I do) there is no need to Put Down One Color and Pick Up The Other, as both colors are poised and ready to be knitted at all times. You may want to experiment with a *knitting thimble*: a wire coil that fits over your index finger with two loops in it through which the two colors run.

If you wish to leave the ends open, the tube may still be worn as a hat or scarf, with your only major decision being the end treatment: garter-stitch, ribbing, a hem, fringes (see ahead for our new I-Cord fringes), or the currently fashionable No Treatment which results in a rolled edge.

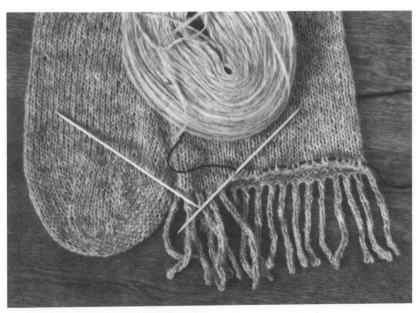

SCARF/HAT

We have made several of these in various weights of wool, and our favorite by far is the single ply, un-spun Icelandic wool - a wheel of which is shown in the photo above. It is very light weight, yet warmer than wool twice its thickness.

SIZE: about 7½" wide (15" circumference) and 55" long. When knitting this loosely, you may work to about 5" shy of total wanted length, as there is plenty of stretch when the finished scarf is wetted and blocked.

MATERIALS: 2 wheels 1-ply Icelandic wool (choose from cream, palest gray, silver gray, steel gray, beige, caramel, dark caramel, or blacksheep), a 16" circular needle (and a set of d.p. needles if you choose the Giant Sock Toe ending) of a size to give you wanted gauge. Approximately #7-10.

GAUGE: 4 stitches to 1"; a loose and open fabric *(see photo on p15)*.

Invisibly **CAST ON** 60 stitches and knit around happily for about 50", adding in color patterns if it pleases you. *(see p23 for Invisible Cast On)*

Ending #1, Giant Toe *(photo, on p15)*: mark off two groups of 6 stitches diametrically opposed to each other. *Knit to within 1 stitch of the first group, K2 tog, K4, SSK. Knit to within 1 stitch of second group, K2 tog, K4, SSK. Knit one round plain. Repeat from * until 28 stitches remain. Divide them onto 2 needles, and weave them together *(see p23)*. Remove the auxiliary thread from the Invisible Casting On, and repeat toe at other end.

Ending #2, I-Cord Fringe *(photo on p15)*: work 2-stitch I-Cord on successive pairs of stitches as follows: with a d.p. needle, *K 2, replace them onto L needle and repeat from * about 20-25 times (depending upon wanted length of fringe). Break wool, thread it through the 2 stitches and finish off. Move on to the next 2 stitches and repeat the foregoing 29 times more. Remove auxiliary thread from Invisible Casting On, and repeat at other end.

(continued on p18)

DUBBELMÖSSA CHART

The tube of the Dubbelmössa is gently narrowed as you approach the summit. Follow the chart. The numbers on the right indicate stitches to be decreased in the plain round before the next pattern begins.

If you are choosing your own charts you will want each pattern to fit exactly into the number of stitches you have on the needle. When adjustments become necessary, cause the number of stitches to be reduced slightly. Begin the chart at the lower right and work to the top of that column; then continue from bottom to top of left column.

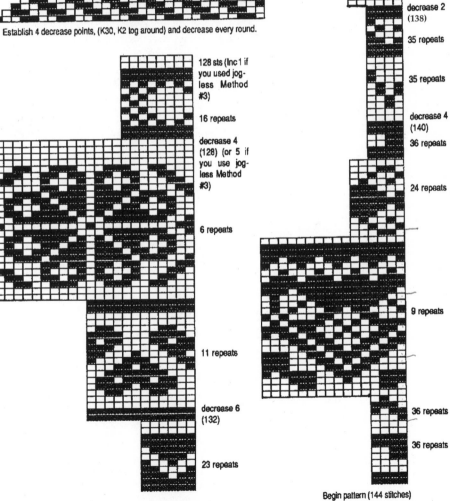

Establish 4 decrease points, (K30, K2 tog around) and decrease every round.

decrease 2
(138)

35 repeats

35 repeats

decrease 4
(140)

36 repeats

24 repeats

128 sts (Inc 1 if you used jog-less Method #3)

16 repeats

decrease 4 (128) (or 5 if you use jog-less Method #3)

6 repeats

9 repeats

11 repeats

decrease 6 (132)

36 repeats

23 repeats

36 repeats

Begin pattern (144 stitches)

From L to R
1-ply unspun
Icelandic at 6½
sts to 1".

Shetland at 6½
sts to 1".

and on the
opposite
page:

Shetland at 6
sts to 1".

wool/angora
blend at
6 sts to 1".

SWEDISH *DUBBELMÖSSA*

SIZE: 24" (or 22") around at widest point

MATERIALS: a total of 5oz Shetland wool; 3oz Main Color (MC), 2oz Contrasting Color (CC). *Or* 2 wheels 1-ply Un-Spun Icelandic wool, one wheel of each color. A 16" circular needle and a set of d.p. needles of a size (approximately #3-5) to give you wanted gauge.

GAUGE: 6 sts to 1" for 24" around, or 6½ sts to 1" for a 22" *Dubbelmössa*.

With 16" needle, Invisibly CAST ON 144 sts in MC. Join, being careful not to twist, and knit around for an inch or so. *(see p23 for Invisible Cast On)*

Introduce the CC and follow the chart on page 17. Note that the cap decreases slightly as it progresses. At the top decrease 1 stitch at each of 4 points equally

spaced around the cap (switching to d.p. needles when necessary). K2 tog will travel to the right; SSK will travel left ... Knitter's Choice. Decrease down to 8 stitches. Break off a yard of both colors and draw through the raw stitches. Twist the yard of wools very tightly, fold it in half and allow it to double back upon itself (leaving a few inches of un-twisted cord at the end). Twist and double again for a shorter cord.

Remove auxiliary wool from the invisible casting on and pick up 144 stitches. Knit in solid color for 2-3" from beginning of pattern. Establish 4 decrease points and K2 tog at each point every 7 rounds, 4 times. Now repeat top shaping in solid color ... you may knit this section in either MC or CC - even adding stripes if you think you will not have sufficient amount of one color for the tassel; no one will see this section. Finish off.

Tassel: (optional, but appearing on all authentic Swedish versions). Wind MC and CC wool around a 5" piece of cardboard (an audio cassette box works well). Tie one end firmly; cut through other end. Wrap and secure the tassel about 3/4" from the tied end. Sew it to the twisted and doubled threads at the top of the cap.

Bits of Esoterica for JOGLESS Color-Pattern KNITTING.

Knitters who do not care for circular knitting are forever harping on the color-jog as one of their main arguments against knitting in the round. They're right ... it is a fact of knitting. However, for the most part, it can be successfully hidden at a side "seam", or down the center front-to-be-cut for a cardigan.

When knitting a yoke-patterned pullover we change colors behind the left shoulder, and can make the dreaded jog all but invisible by neatly darning in the ends: pulling the end of the first stitch of a new color **Up** and to the **Right,** and the tail of the last stitch of the color **Down** and to the **Left**. The success of this technique is dependent upon the will-power of the knitter: you must have resisted all temptation to carry an unused color up a few rounds to where you will need it again ... **break it off, leaving a sufficient darning-in tail**.

Next Method: when knitting a color pattern that consists of separated motifs (such as OXO in Fair Isle, or a Norwegian star, etc), you may entirely defeat the jog by floating the first stitch of each round, and permitting it to travel between the motifs. This will eliminate a jog in the motif itself, and merely cause a difference in the number of stitches between the first and last patterns (if floating to the right), or the first and second patterns (if floating to the left) ... un-noticeable to the point that you may defy even the most eagle-eyed knitter to spot where you began each round.

Method #3 is only applicable to certain patterns. An example is the diamond pattern at the top of the chart on page 17. Here it behooves you to DECrease one stitch in the first round for a multiple of 2 minus 1; try it and see.

Method #4: this is a brand-new technique that I came up with a few weeks ago. Irritated excessively by the noticeable jog that occurs in solid stripes of color, I began messing about, and stumbled upon a technique new to me. It combines the Floating First Stitch idea with a Knitting-Into-the-Stitch-of-the-Row-Below move. Grab a circular sampler so you can knit along.

Knit 2 rounds of the background color plain. Now you want to knit two rounds of a CC: knit the entire first round of CC, then - with the first stitch of the new color on the

This photo shows an Old Jogged hat on the L, and the New Improved Jogless hat on the R. The straight needle indicates the beginning of the

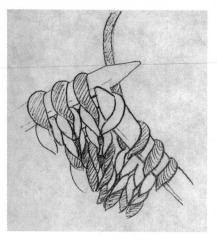

L needle, pick up the right side of the stitch of the row below and put it (untwisted) onto the L needle next to the first stitch. Knit those 2 strands together. This will cause the "first" stitch to move one stitch to the left, because the thread lifted from below will completely cover the original first stitch of CC. Do nothing further until you want to change color again. If you do a series of solid stripes, your "first" stitch may move (one stitch at a time) 4 or 5 stitches to the left. You can usually lurch back to your **real** first stitch all at once if you arrange matters so that the next color pattern begins with 4 or 5 stitches of the background color. Now take a look at the color joins ... no jog, and no need to break off the wool not in use.

To fold a traditional *Dubbelmössa*, going clockwise from top L: *a.* full extension. *b.* plain section pushed in (*it may be worn this way as a long stocking cap*). *c.* main pattern pushed in. *d.* main pattern turned up; four thicknesses over forehead and ears; ready to take on arctic conditions.

A few techniques

Two methods of Invisible Casting On 1. Using auxiliary wool and a crochet hook, make a crochet chain of about 4-5 stitches *more* than the number of stitches you want to cast on. The top side of the finished chain looks like a strip of hearts ... turn it over and, using MC and skipping the first few, knit up 1 stitch into each purl bump on the **back** of the hearts. Ignore the extras at the beginning and end. When the scarf or hat is finished, simply un-zip the crochet chain to reveal raw stitches waiting to be picked up and knitted in the opposite direction. (Slicker version: chain a few sts, then crochet wanted number of stitches directly over and onto the needle. Chain a few more off the needle.)

OR:

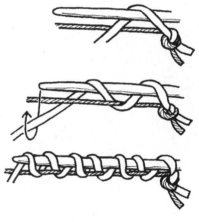

2. Loosely knot together the working wool *(the thick strand in the drawings)* and a spare bit of wool. Holding the knot in your right hand - along with the needle - follow the steps in the drawing: pick up the working wool from in front of the spare wool, then from behind the spare wool. When you need the stitches again, simply   un-tie the knot and pull out the spare wool - revealing the patiently waiting stitches.

To weave the Giant Sock Toe, use **Stocking-Stitch Weaving** shown here. This may be worked on or off the needles. Be sure to use a **blunt** sewing-up needle to prevent splitting the wool.

CHAPTER THREE

Spiral Yoke Sweater

March 1992. Dear Knitter,

When Elizabeth held up this design of mine during the filming of the *Knitting Workshop* series, it was to show one of the many possibilities of an **EPS** yoke sweater. We had a minor deluge of enquires for instructions and, surprisingly, the requests have maintained a gratifyingly steady, if somewhat modest flow ever since. So we have pulled ourselves together to supply you with proper directions.

The garment is mostly an **EPS** (*Elizabeth's Percentage System*, see Knitting Workshop) seamless yoke construction: your personal GAUGE times wanted circumference at widest body part (*parts is parts*) equals the Key Number [K]. Nearly all other calculations will be a percentage of [K]. The biggest difference from basic EPS in the following Spiral Yoke design, is that instead of

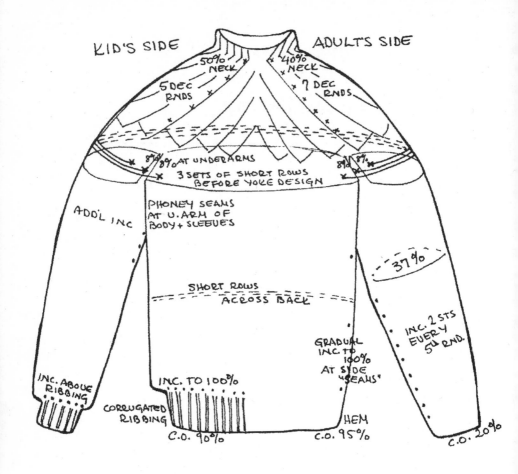

KID'S SIDE   ADULT'S SIDE

50% NECK   40% NECK

5 DEC RNDS   7 DEC RNDS.

8% 8% AT UNDERARMS   8% 8%

3 SETS OF SHORT ROWS BEFORE YOKE DESIGN

ADD'L INC

PHONEY SEAMS AT U. ARM OF BODY + SLEEVES

37%

SHORT ROWS ACROSS BACK

INC. 2 STS EVERY 5ᵗʰ RND.

GRADUAL INC. TO 100% AT SIDE "SEAMS"

INC. ABOVE RIBBING

INC. TO 100%

CORRUGATED RIBBING

HEM

C.O. 90%   C.O. 95%   C.O. 20%

the standard *three* yoke-decrease rounds, you will have *five* for the kid's and *seven* for the adult's version.

The yoke shaping is spaced between the spiral lines; so the number of stitches reduced in each decrease round is dependent upon how many spirals you have established. When deciding upon the number of spirals, keep in mind that you want the lines to meet at the neck ... in other words, the number of plain stitches separating the spirals is going to be reduced to one stitch. You may spiral clockwise or anti-clockwise as your individual vortex field requires. I have knitted one of each for you. The kid's version has corrugated ribbing at the lower edges and a 2-color spiral; the adult's version has hems and a Travelling Stitch spiral. Either one may end with a turtleneck (as in the prototype), a crew neck (kid's model) or reverse spiral crew (as knitted in the video). Since the pattern precludes us from raising the neck-back at the top, we raised it just before the yoke pattern began. At our gauge, three sets of Short Rows will do the trick for an adult size; two sets for the kid's size.

Yoke Shaping: count the total sleeve and body stitches on the needle. Decide upon wanted width between points of the spiral pattern. Does the pattern repeat number divide into your yoke stitches? If not, you may fudge a few stitches up or down - but if the fudge is too great, alter the spiral's width.

Next, consider that lovely plain body to be a gigantic swatch and count your row gauge. EPS tells us that the yoke depth is one-quarter of the circumference in inches; and Medrith Glover adds that a yoke rarely (if ever) is deeper than 10" no matter how voluminous the body. But for circumferences up to 40-42", the 25% - in inches - applies.

Multiply the row gauge times inches of yoke depth, and that us the number of rows with which you have to play.

Now calculate the number of stitches you will have left at the neck (40% of [K] for adults, 50% of [K] for children). Divide the total number of rows roughly by 5 (child's size), or 7 (adult's size) and decrease between each spiral in each of those 5 or 7 rounds. Double check your math; you should end up with close to the final wanted number of neck stitches. **OR**, proceed to the specific instructions that follow.

KID'S SPIRAL YOKE, 2-color version

SIZE: 27" around body. Length is up to you - but about 13" to under-arm for a 6-8 year old kid.

GAUGE: 4½ stitches and 6½ rows to 1". 4½ times 27" = 122, or [K].

MATERIALS: only two 4oz skeins of Maritime Blue *Homespun* wool (B), 1 skein Cream (C) *Homespun* (or 2oz of something you have on hand of the same weight). A 24" circular, and a set of d.p. needles of a size to give you wanted gauge: about #5-7.

Body: with 24" needle, and B wool, CAST ON 108 stitches (89% of [K]). K1, P1 in B for 1 round.

Corrugated Rib: K1C, P1B for 2". Knit 1 round in B and increase to [K] (122 stitches) by working **K7, M1** 4 times, then **K8, M1** 10 times. Work 4" plain. Insert a set of Short Rows *(see p34)* across the lack only (optional) to prevent the dreaded riding-up. Work Phoney Seams *(see p35)* at sides (optional also). Put body aside.

Sleeve: on d.p. needles **Cast On** about 20% of [K] (26 stitches). Work corrugated Rib as above for 2". Increase severely in next round: K2, M1 around (39 stitches). Work straight for about 5". Mark 3 underarm stitches and INcrease 1 stitch each side of 3 marked stitches every 7th round 3 times (37% of [K], 45 stitches). Work straight to wanted length (about 14"), erring a bit on the too-long side because kid's arms don't get any shorter, and this is a slightly bloused sleeve style. Make second sleeve. Work Phoney Seams down center of the 3 marked stitches if wanted.

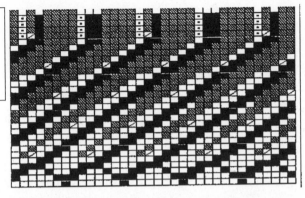

White boxes = MC
Black boxes = CC
Grey boxes = non-existent (decreased) stitches.
/= K 2 together

Underarms: put 8% of [K] (9 sts) onto threads at each underarm of both body and sleeves, carefully centered above the *seam* stitches.

Unite the sleeves to the body - matching underarms. All stitches (176) are now on the

24" needle. Knit 3 rounds on all stitches.

Back-of-Neck Shaping: K5 stitches past left front underarm join. *Wrap, turn, work (either by Purling, or by Knitting Back Backward) to corresponding point on right front. Wrap, turn, knit to 5 stitches shy of 1st Wrap. Repeat from * 2 times more for a total of 6 extra rows (3 sets of Short Rows). Knit around on all stitches, working the Wraps together with their slipped stitches. *(see p34 for more detail on "wrapping")*

Pattern: begin behind L shoulder. The chart is a 7-stitch repeat and divides into 176 25 times with 1 leftover. Do not get rid of that extra stitch; it is critical to produce a Jogless yoke pattern. Your "first" pattern stitch will float to the right following the spiral (i.e. you will re-assign it at the beginning of each round). This will make more sense when you are there. *(see p35)*

Yoke Decreases: because there are 25 spirals, you will be eliminating 25 stitches in each decrease-round. There will be 4 rounds between each dec round (except the last time) as follows: after 9 rounds from the union of sleeves and body (count in front, not the Short Rows), decrease 1 stitch (k2 tog) between each spiral as indicated on chart (151 stitches). K 4 rounds.

Second Decrease: eats up 25 more stitches = 126 remaining. Knit 4 rounds.

Third Decrease: minus 25 stitches = 101 remaining. K 4 rounds.

Fourth Decrease: minus 25 stitches - 76 stitches. Knit 4 rounds.

Final (partial) Decrease and Crew-Neck: turn 6 stitches into 5 by *K2C, P1B, K2 tog C, P1B. Repeat from * around. 63 stitches remain. Now, • K2C, P1B, K1C, P1B. Repeat from • a total of 3 rounds. K 1 round in B and CAST OFF loosely in B, using Elizabeth's *Sewn Cast Off (see p35)* for an elastic selvedge.

Weave underarms *(see p81)*. Darn in ends. Block.

ADULT'S SPIRAL YOKE,
Travelling Stitch Version

SIZE: 42" around. Length is up to you.

GAUGE: 4½ stitches and 6½ rows to 1". 4½ times 42" = 190 (really 189, but round off), or [K].

MATERIALS: 5, 4oz skeins Cream Homespun wool. 16" and 24" circular, and a set of d.p. needles of a size to give you wanted gauge (approximately #5-7).

This version begins with a hem *(naturally you may*

switch this to ribbing if you prefer) which is worked last to prevent an inelastic cast-on or -off edge. To facilitate knitting-up the hem at the

end, begin with Long Tail Casting On (see p35) and consider the outline-stitch side to be the "right" side.

Body: Cast On 178 stitches. Join (untwisted) and mark "seam" stitches at each side (88 stitches apart) with Coilless Pins. After 3", increase at each side seam as follows: K to within 1 stitch of marker, M1, K3, M1. Repeat at other side. Knit another 3-4" and repeat. After 3 sets of increases you will be up to 190 stitches or 100% [K]. Insert a set of Short Rows (see p34) at the halfway point if you wish to obviate the Dreaded Riding Up syndrome. Knit to wanted length to underarm. Work a Phony Seam on the side "seam" stitches (optional; see p35). Put 8% of [K] (15 stitches) on threads at underarms, carefully centered above the "seam" stitches.

Sleeve: with d.p. needles, CAST ON about 20% of [K] (40 stitches). Mark center 3 stitches and Increase 1 stitch each side of them every 5th round to 37% of [K] (70 stitches). Work straight to wanted length to underarm. Put 8% of [K] (15 stitches) on a thread at the underarm, carefully centered above the marked stitches.

Unite body and sleeves: 190 body stitches + 70 + 70, minus 60 underarm stitches = 270 Yoke stitches ÷ 10 stitches for each spiral pattern (K8, LT), = 27 spirals around the yoke. Work 3 or 4 rounds on all stitches.

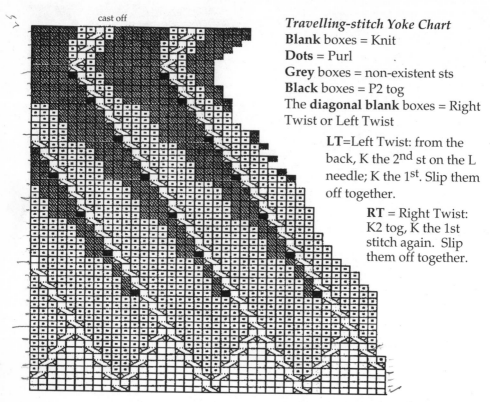

cast off

Travelling-stitch Yoke Chart
Blank boxes = Knit
Dots = Purl
Grey boxes = non-existent sts
Black boxes = P2 tog
The **diagonal blank** boxes = Right Twist or Left Twist

LT=Left Twist: from the back, K the 2nd st on the L needle; K the 1st. Slip them off together.

RT = Right Twist: K2 tog, K the 1st stitch again. Slip them off together.

Yoke shaping: a 9½" deep yoke at 6½ rows to 1" = about 60+ rounds into which to fit the shaping which will result in a 40% of [K] neck opening.

Begin with 3 sets of Short Rows to raise the back of the neck as follows: Knit to 7 stitches past the sleeve join at L front. Wrap, turn, and work back to the corresponding point on the R front. *Wrap, turn and work back to 5 stitches shy of 1st wrap. Repeat from * for a total of 6 rows (3 sets). Knit one round on all stitches, knitting the wraps together with the slipped stitches. *(See Short Rows and Wrapping on pages 34 for more details.)*

Yoke Pattern (in travelling stitch): follow the chart on the preceding page. At 18-20 rounds from the sleeve union (count in front; not the short rows), work the ...

FIRST decrease by purling 2 together between the spiral lines. Keep the decrease right next to the travelling stitch for less visibility. You will get rid of 27 stitches and now have 243. Knit 5 rounds.

SECOND decrease: gets rid of 27 stitches = 216. Work 5 rounds.

THIRD decrease: minus 27 stitches = 189. Work 5 rounds.

FOURTH decrease: minus 27 stitches = 162 stitches. Work 5 rounds.

FIFTH decrease: minus 27 stitches = 135 stitches. Work 5 rounds.

SIXTH decrease: minus 27 stitches = 108 stitches. Work 3 rounds.

SEVENTH decrease: minus 27 stitches = 81 stitches. Aha! we're there. 40% of [K] = 76 stitches ... close enough. Work 1 more round. Now reverse the travelling stitches from L-twist to R-twist, and work another 5 rounds for neck edge - or continue on to a mock- or a full-turtleneck if you like. Cast off loosely. Elizabeth's Sewn Casting Off is recommended *(see p35)*.

Hem - Body: knit up 1 stitch for each cast-on stitch around the lower edge ... knitting into the purl bumps behind the outline stitch. Switch to a lighter weight wool and knit around for the hem - adding a color pattern, or knitting in a secret message if you wish. If you cannot find any lighter-weight wool lying about, decrease 10% on the second round (K8, K2 tog). If using a contrasting color, work the last round in the body color. Slide about 10-15 stitches off the needle at a time, and, with a sharp sewing-up needle, neatly (and loosely) sew them down - skimming the needle through the surface of the body, then through the raw stitch. Be sure to keep the stitching in the same horizontal row all around.

Hem - Sleeves: we were going to put hems in the sleeve cuffs, but the selvedge showed little inclination to curl, so we changed our mind. We picked up all stitches around the cuff and used two applications of Elizabeth's Sewn Casting Off *(see next page)* to give it stability ... and very nice it looks, too. You may do either, or neither.

Weave the underarm stitches. On a yoke-style sweater there is invariably a distressing hole at each end.

To obviate this, slide the stitches-to-be-woven onto a *body* and a *sleeve* d.p. needle. You will now see some sloppy threads at the ends. Pick up a loose strand, twist it into a stitch and add it to

8-year old twins Wade *(in the original turtleneck)* and Adam Caflisch live down the road from Schoolhouse Press.

the needle. Repeat the foregoing at each end of both needles - adding two stitches to each needle - and weave them to each other. This is usually sufficient, but if a small hole remains you may cover it with a duplicate stitch. *(Drawing of Weaving on p23)*

More TECHNIQUES

Short Rows & Wrapping, Part 1: at turning point leave the working wool where it is (in back if you're knitting; in front if you're purling), slip the next stitch to the R needle. Bring the wool to the other side and replace the slipped stitch to L needle. Now you are ready to work back to the point of the corresponding wrap. **Part 2**: when next you meet the wrapped stitch, work both the wrap and the slipped stitch together as one. Magic.

Extra Stitch in 2-color yoke pattern: essentially we have a *Wrinkle in Time* ... that extra stitch - when spiralling to the right - is a phantom, but necessary to have the finished pattern appear to be symmetrical. If you decide to spiral to the left, you will need a multiple of **7 minus** 1 ... don't ask, just rejoice that it works so beautifully. Since it is all but unnoticeable in the travelling-stitch version, we left it alone to fend for itself.

The **Phoney Seam** *(top, right)*: drop the center sleeve or body stitch off the needle and cause it to "run" to just above the lower ribbing. With a crochet hook, grab the stitch and hook it up at a different rate: *hook up two ladders together, then one ladder. Repeat from *. This means the resulting stitch has one-third fewer rounds that its neighboring stitches causing a subtle welt.

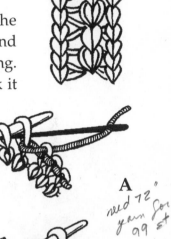

A

need 72" for yarn for 99 st

B

Elizabeth Zimmermann's **Sewn Casting Off** provides a surprisingly elastic selvedge. With a blunt needle, *A.* *go through the first 2 stitches from R to L. *B.* go back through the first stitch from L to R, slip 1st stitch off needle and pull wool through. Repeat from *.

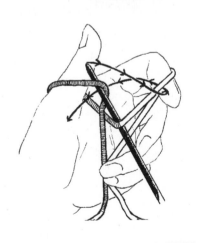

Terminology is confusing: **Long-Tail Casting On** is sometimes referred to as Single Needle, or Two Strand casting on. It is very fast to execute and yields an outline-stitch on one side and purl bumps on the other.

CHAPTER FOUR

Mañanita

Sept '92. Dear Knitter,

Remember when waves of Guernseys, Entrelac and Fair Isle sweaters swept across the knitting landscape - each in their turn? We feel that Lace Knitting will be the next discipline to capture the collective knitting consciousness. No longer are lace shawls relegated to "old ladies", but are now seen as dramatic and romantic Fashion Statements draped over women of all ages. To the existing shawl-shapes of circle, square, triangle, horseshoe and oblong, we now add the *Mañanita*.

LACE - the very word exudes an aura of mystery and advanced knowledge. But we liken knitting lace to making a soufflé: once executed you realize that each is mostly air, and really no trick at all. If you can increase by means of Yarn Over, and cause a decrease to lean L, R

37

or go straight, you have all the rudiments of lace knitting at your needle tips. And - if you can make a cream sauce and fold in beaten egg whites, you have a soufflé.

When perusing your lace books in search of an appropriate pattern or recipe, do not overlook doilies and tablecloths. A pillow cover knitted on #0000 needles may be converted into a full size shawl by working the identical set of instructions on #15 needles. *(photo below)*

As proof that we lace knitters (not a particularly vociferous group) are gradually being heard, we note more and more books and magazine articles being

devoted to lace knitting. We are especially pleased to see that most lace designs are charted. Even though we have not achieved a universal chart-symbol system, there are usually only 6-8 symbols to memorize for any given pattern - and the ability to *see* the design offsets the minor annoyance of having to learn a new symbol system with each new book.

Just as we were first writing out the instructions for this "new" lace garment (we had never seen one before), and were wondering what to call it, we learned that it is a familiar garment in Mexico, called a *Mañanita* - which translates, romantically, into "pretty little morning". They are knitted in varying lengths, from very short to a more dramatic knee-length. We find several great advantages to this type of "shawl" ... a regular circular or square shawl must be folded over for wear often obliterating the delicate lace design - whereas the Mañanita is a single layer all around, and you do not have to clutch, tie or pin this garment to keep it in place.

If you are new to lace knitting, this *Mañanita* is an excellent place to begin, as it eliminates the only tricky bit of knitting a closed circle: the beginning - which involves casting 6-10 stitches onto 3 or 4 double-pointed needles. This is often a slithery bit of business, with needles plummeting to the floor left and right.

*TWO TIPS for coping with this difficulty: use wooden or bamboo d.p. needles as the wool will stick to them - or master Beverly Royce's technique in her book, **Notes on Double Knitting**, and work the first few inches in that mode - back and forth on 2 needles - until enough stitches have been increased to slide right onto a 16" or 24" circular needle.*

The necessary techniques to work the charts on pages 40, 41 are relatively simple: increase by means of Yarn Over (YO; duck the R needle under working wool), and left (SSK) or right (K2 tog) leaning decreases, plus a double decrease (Slip 1, K2 tog, psso).

(continued on p42)

The taradiddles across the top indicate stitches to be gathered together for a crochet-loop edge. *(see p45)*

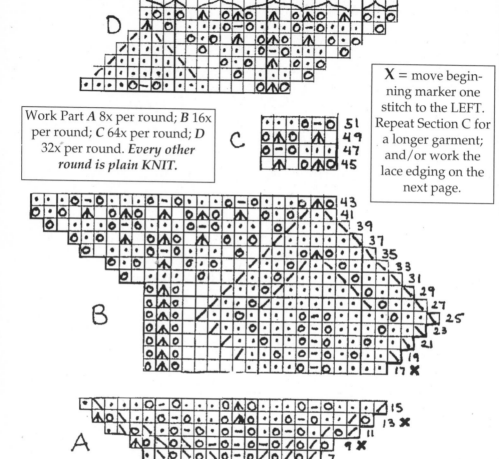

D

Work Part *A* 8x per round; *B* 16x per round; *C* 64x per round; *D* 32x per round. *Every other round is plain KNIT.*

C

X = move beginning marker one stitch to the LEFT. Repeat Section C for a longer garment; and/or work the lace edging on the next page.

51
49
47
45

43
41
39
37
35
33
31
29
27
25
23
21
19
17 **X**

B

15
13 **X**
11
9 **X**
7

A

PRIMULA: Cast On 84 stitches. Knit one round plain.
Round 1. YO, K2 tog around. **Rounds 2 & 3.** Plain Knit. **Round 4.** *K1, YO, K2 tog, YO. Repeat from * around (112 stitches). **Rounds 5 & 6.** Plain Knit. **Now go to line 7 on the chart above.**

The above is a portion of the Primula design from Marianne Kinzel's *First Book of Modern Lace Knitting (Dover Publications)*. Section D is something Meg added to lengthen the garment, and is not part of M. Kinzel's design.

We also knitted a version that ended after Section C; shorter and very pretty. Since you cannot easily hide a darned-in end in lace, *splice* in each new skein of wool *(see p44)*.

Repeat each line 10x per round to the **star**, then 20x per round to the top. **Every other round is KNIT (not shown on chart).** "OOO" = triple yarn over. On following round, K 18 stitches into the OOO of previous round (K1, P1 3x into each of the 3 YOs). This does not appear on the chart as it occurs on a plain K round.

Turn this page sideways. **Ignore the blank squares; they simply define the design and have no other meaning.**

ı =	Knit
— =	Knit 1 back
O =	Yarn Over
/ =	Knit 2 together
**** =	SSK (slip, slip, knit)
Λ =	Slip 1, K 2 tog, psso
V =	K1, P1 into same st.
ооо =	Triple Yarn Over
18 b =	K in *back* of newly-made 18 sts.

Knit one more round plain. Shawl done. Invisibly Cast On 5 stitches and begin Lace Border (*charted below*)

Cast On 80, K 1 rnd.

Begin Chart

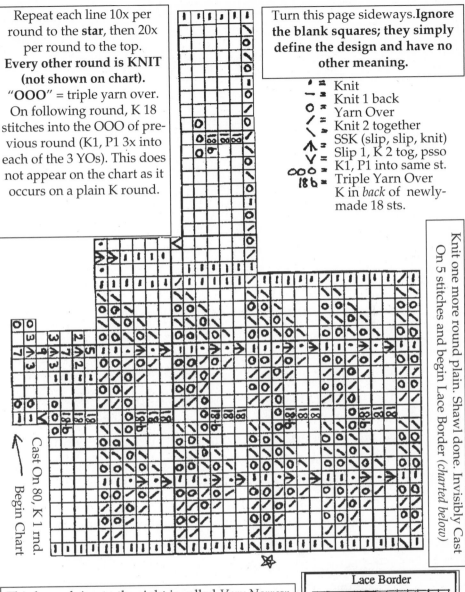

This lace edging to the right is called *Very Narrow Eyelet Edging* from **Barbara Abbey's Knitting Lace** (*Schoolhouse Press*); charted by Meg.

The *squiggle* at the ends of every even-numbered row = unite last lace-border stitch to a raw shawl stitch. *S* = slip, + = purl, and the *shaded squares* at the beginning of Row 8 are non-existent (cast off) stitches.

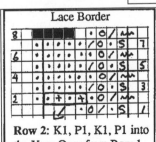

Lace Border

Row 2: K1, P1, K1, P1 into the Yarn Over from Row 1.
Row 8: Cast Off first 4 sts.

The chart on page 41:
We have named this pattern *Peacock*. Meg adapted it from a (nameless) small table-center by Austrian lace-designer Herbert Neibling. She had received a rudimentary - typewriter adapted - chart of the pattern from Thom Christoph many years ago.

Our *Mañanita*s begin easily on a 16" circular needle with 80-90 stitches (about 27" to 34" center circumference, or a 8½" to 10¾" diameter neck opening, and in a few inches you may slide comfortably onto a 24" needle on which you will remain to the end.

The final border presents you with the choice of a fairly speedily-completed crochet loop edging, or a more elegant sideways lace finish.

Gauge is not too critical for this garment. Your main concern is to have the center opening as wide as you want ... choosing between a relatively high heck, a scooped neck, or perhaps an off-the-shoulder deal. Remember: a too large neck may easily be cinched in by the final I-Cord edging; a too tight neck will remain too tight. Length is also something you will have to take an educated guess about. When knitting fine wool on large needles, it is difficult to determine the final blocked dimensions of the poncho. Our Peacock version came off the needles measuring a shrivelled 15" from neck to border. Upon being blocked, it metamorphized to 24" (*see photo on p38*). To get a close idea of length while the stitches are still on the needle: grab the cast-on edge in one hand, and the working needle in the other. Pull the knitting ruthlessly taut, and get someone to measure the distance between your hands.

If you are transforming a doily into a shawl using #15 needles, we advise using the un-spun Icelandic wool for needles that large. Using Shetland or Icelandic Laceweight on #15's causes the finished work to resemble chicken wire - whereas the soft hairiness of un-spun Icelandic fills in the holes somewhat. Also, unspun Icelandic is the warmest of all other lightweight wools; that fuzzy halo is very efficient at trapping body heat. OK, let's cast on.

SIZE: approximately 15" unblocked; 24" blocked from neck to lower edge. Neck opening anywhere from 26-35" circumference (ours is 34" on #10 needles).

MATERIALS: two 100 gram skeins of *Icelandic Laceweight* (natural colors of Cream, Pale Grey, Beige, or dyed shades of Sky Blue, Medium Blue, Navy Blue, Brick Red, Cranberry Red or Charcoal Grey ... these are not pastels, but very bold colors.) *OR* 6oz *Shetland Laceweight* (White, Cream, silvery Grey, Soft Beige, Cornflower Blue, Bressay Blue, dusty Rose or Black), *OR* 8oz *Shetland Jumper Weight* (choose from 68 colors), *OR* 3 wheels *Un Spun Icelandic* (choose from 8 natural, undyed shades). A 16" and 24" circular needle, size anywhere from #10 to #15.

Reading Charts: you will find yourself quickly memorizing the symbols. Follow the charts in the same manner as a color-pattern, but **the blank spaces are nothings** ... they are simply there to enable the pattern-maker to visually articulate the design. Begin reading the chart at the lower R corner. Read from R to L. Repeat each line as many times as indicated. Tie a bit of brightly colored wool on your needle to mark the beginning of the round. If you feel a bit insecure, tie a second color loop after each pattern repeat. then, if you have veered off track, you will notice right away and can quickly find the error in a single repeat and not have to rip an entire round.

In the *Primula,* pay attention to the **X** indicating a shift in the first stitch of the round. Parts A, B and C of the *Primula* were designed by Marianne Kinzel, and are taken from her book, *The First Book of Modern Lace Knitting (Dover Publications)*. Section D is something we added to lengthen the garment a bit. We also knitted a version that ended after section C ... shorter and very pretty. Knitter's choice. For crochet edging, see next page.

Splicing: Since you cannot easily hide a darned-in end in lace, splice in each new skein of wool. For 2-ply **Shetland Laceweight**: separate ends into their component plies. Break off about 3" of one of the plies from each end. Overlap the strands onto one palm; lick the other palm and rub your hands together. We call this a Spit-Splice *(see p10)*. For **1-ply unspun Icelandic**, draw out the old and new ends to reduce the thickness. Overlap and spit-splice (SS) as above. For the **1-ply spun Icelandic Laceweight**, un-spin a 3" section of each end. Draw out the strands as above, and S.S.

FINISHING

Peacock Sideways Lace edging: upon completing

At the end of a border-row, K2 together through back loops - being the last lace stitch and one stitch-to-be-cast-off.

the final round (400 stitches), Invisibly Cast On *(see p23)* 5 stitches. Turn. Knit 5, work the last stitch together with a raw stitch. Turn. Begin row 1 of chart on page 41. Work back and forth, uniting the end of every other row (2, 4, 6, and 8) to a raw stitch by whatever means you prefer: K2 tog, SSK, K2 tog tbl, or Sl 1, K1, psso. With 400 stitches and an 8-row border repeat, you should be able to fit 100 repeats in evenly. Remove auxiliary thread from Invisible Cast On, rip out the first "free" knit row, and weave the end to the beginning using garter-stitch weaving. *(see p81)*

Primula crochet edging: follow the taradiddles on page 40. On a 16-stitch pattern repeat, shift the first stitch to the R needle. *Gather 2 stitches together, and work 9 chains, (gather 3 stitches, 9 crochet chains) repeat between ( ) 3x. Then 2 stitches 6 chains, 3 stitches 6 chains. Repeat from * around edge.

The **Neck Edge** may easily be adjusted by the final application of I-Cord to the cast on selvedge. Try the garment on after blocking. We hope that it will either be just right, or too large... if just right, work Elizabeth's Applied I-Cord border *(p46)* on the same size needles. If the opening is too large, work with a smaller needle.

Applied I-Cord is worked as follows: pick up 1 stitch for each cast-on stitch around the neck edge. Cast on 2 stitches and transfer them to the pick-up needle. *K1, K2 tog tbl (being the last Cord stitch and one picked-up stitch. Replace the 2 stitches to the L needle, and repeat from * all around. Weave end to beginning. (For a slightly thicker edge, you may work with 3 Cord stitches: K2, K2 tog tbl, replace.)

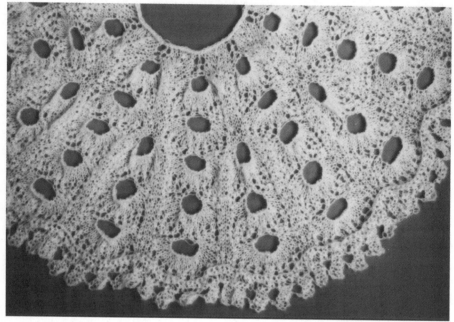

An un-blocked Mañanita

Blocking: wash the *Mañanita* in cool water. Rinse. Squeeze out the excess water. wrap it in a bath towel and jump on it. Now vacuum a circle on the rug and flop the damp shawl down. Grab a box of T-pins and stretch-and-pin out the halves, quarters, eighth, sixteenths, etc. You may stretch it quite severely - like unto a guitar string - the wool can take it. The more loosely it was knitted, the greater the blocked growth will be. Naturally, if it looks as if it's coming out to be too large, you may block it more gently. It should dry in a matter of hours.

The shrivelled lace shown in the photo on the preceding page will become transformed into the beautifully "dressed" lace shown below.

CHAPTER FIVE

I-Cord Finger Gloves

March, 1990. Dear Knitter,

Perhaps you have avoided knitting gloves for the same reasons we have all these years:

A. Working the skinny little fingers on tiny double-pointed needles has little appeal ... plus, when one finger is finished it will get in the way of the subsequent ones (I suppose you could poke the finished fingers inside).

B. Double-knitted gloves with their anatomical

shaping (á la Beverly Royce's wonderful book, *Notes on Double Knitting*) remain a mystery to us.

    C. Sideways garter-stitch gloves are easy enough to execute, but the results are quite klutzy, unless knitted

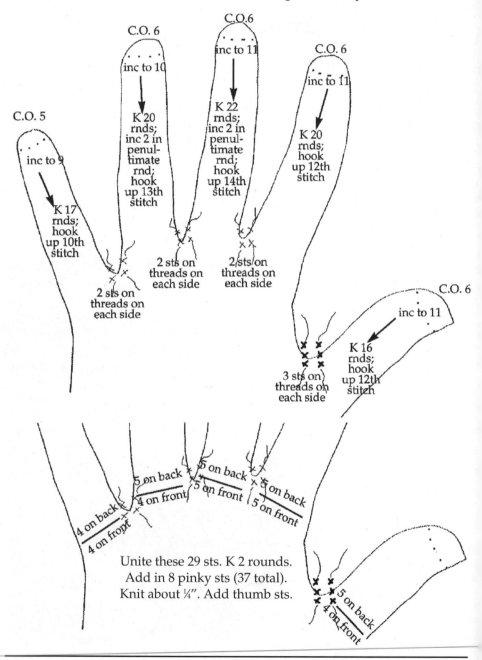

C.O. 6

inc to 10

K 20 rnds; inc 2 in penultimate rnd; hook up 13th stitch

C.O.6

inc to 11

K 22 rnds; inc 2 in penultimate rnd; hook up 14th stitch

C.O. 6

inc to 11

K 20 rnds; hook up 12th stitch

C.O. 5

inc to 9

K 17 rnds; hook up 10th stitch

2 sts on threads on each side

2 sts on threads on each side

2 sts on threads on each side

C.O. 6

inc to 11

K 16 rnds; hook up 12th stitch

3 sts on threads on each side

5 on back
4 on front

4 on back
4 on front

5 on back
5 on front

5 on back
5 on front

5 on back
5 on front

5 on back
4 on front

Unite these 29 sts. K 2 rounds.
Add in 8 pinky sts (37 total).
Knit about ¼". Add thumb sts.

in fine Shetland Wool; then they are not warm enough.

While ruminating about I-Cord one day we realized that we used mostly 2 or 3 stitch Cord *(see p81)*. You may have already tried a 4-stitch I-Cord ... it works, but might look a bit sloppy where the wool is carried across the back.

OK. what about a 6, or 8, or 10-stitch I-Cord? Yes, the sloppy bit will become a veritable ladder across the back.

Try this: Cast On a 10-stitch I-Cord and knit until the tube is about as long as your forefinger. Take your trusty crochet hook, and hook the ladder up into an eleventh stitch! N.B. while working the 10-stitch Cord, do not pull the wool too snugly across the back. If you have ever worked a Phony Seam you will have noted (after dropping the "seam" stitch) how inordinately long the ladders appeared to be. It takes more wool to make a stitch that you realize, so be sure to allow a stitches-worth of wool in your I-Cord ladder (approximately ⅝ to ¾" in a 5-stitches-to-1"-weight wool).

We tried casting on Invisibly at the base of the fingers, but find we prefer beginning at the top with fewer stitches and increasing in the 2nd or 3rd round to give a rudimentary Finger Shape. When finger-length is achieved, place the raw stitches on a thread, twist the finger-tip-rung of the ladder into a stitch, hook it up (down, actually) to the bottom as if repairing a dropped stitch. Put this additional stitch on the thread and cast on for the next finger.

The most crucial measurement is the circumference of the palm (7½" for us). Multiply this times your gauge (7½" x 5 stitches to 1" = 37 stitches), and that resulting number is what you must achieve after leaving the finger-gusset stitches on threads, and uniting the fingers. *(see drawing on p50)*

For decisions about the circumference of each finger, check the recipients hand. Our thumb, index and middle fingers are all approximately the same circumference (2½"), so we only alter the number for the ring and little fingers. After all, this is knitting! Measure, or try on, for wanted lengths.

We like to knit all 10 digits consecutively, as they work up so quickly, and you can make sure each pair of fingers and thumbs match each other. It helps to put them on the arm of your knitting chair in proper order as they are knitted, and see that they are not disturbed until you are ready to unite them. (Beware of small animals and children.)

Now then, this is the only really tricky part: with a set of double-pointed needles, pick up the stitches around the base of the fingers EXCEPT for two "crotch" stitches at *each side* of the middle and ring fingers, and the *inner sides only* of the index and little fingers. These will later be woven to each other.

To achieve a most anatomical fit, unite the first 3 fingers; work for 2 rounds, **then** join in the little finger. (To prove the necessity for this, turn your open palm toward yourself with the fingers together ... see how the base of the little finger is lower than the others?

Naturally, there will be those to whom the above does not apply; proceed as required.) Upon joining in the little finger, you should have your wanted number of palm stitches (37 for me).

Work around for about 2". Try on the fingers and determine if it is time to add the thumb.

You now have the option of a Palm Thumb or a Side Thumb. The side thumb offers the advantage of making the gloves ambidextrous, but place it wherever you like.

At your chosen location, put 3 palm stitches, and 3 thumb stitches on threads; knit around the base of the thumb and onward ... not unlike uniting the sleeve to the yoke of a (tiny) sweater.

Another option presents itself here: what kind of a thumb gusset shape would you like? Straight down the middle? or beginning at the thumb-corners and veering inward until the shaping lines meet at the wrist? Knitters choice. *(Instructions for both will follow.)*

At wrist length you may want to switch to ribbing for 3-4" and cast off. OR you might choose to nip in for the wrist by decreasing all around, knitting for 1", then increasing again for a gauntlet.

Cast off, weave finger gussets, darn in ends.

I-CORD GLOVE DETAILS FOR DOUBTING KNITTERS

SIZE: 7½" palm circumference
GAUGE: 5 stitches to 1"
MATERIALS: 1 3½oz skein MC in *Québécoise* or *Homespun* or any wool that will give you wanted gauge; 2oz CC if patterned gauntlet is chosen. A set of double-pointed needles (approximately #4-5), 11½" circular needle for gauntlet and a crochet hook.

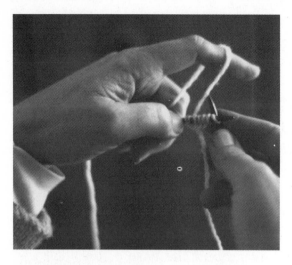

I-Cord Pinky: *(make 2)* On d.p. needle, CAST ON 5 stitches. Do not turn, but slide stitches to other end of needle and knit them. All fingers will be worked in this non-turning mode - which is I-Cord. *(See photo above: the wool is coming from the last stitch to be drawn across the back and knitted to the first stitch.)*

Next round: *K into the back of the stitch of the row below (increase), K1. Repeat from * 4 times, K last stitch (9 stitches total). Work in I-Cord for 17 rounds - or wanted length.

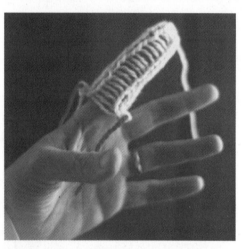

With crochet hook, twist finger-tip ladder into a stitch and hook up (down) each ladder to the bottom *(photo below)*. Put all 10 raw stitches on a thread *(photo next page)*.

I-Cord Ring Finger: *(make 2)* Cast On 6 stitches. Work as for pinky, increasing to 10 stitches in 2nd round. Work for 20 rounds, BUT on the 19th round, increase 2 stitches - one at each side - for gussets between fingers *(drawing on p50)*

Hook up ladder. Put all 13 stitches on a thread.

I-Cord Middle Finger: *(make 2)* Cast On 6 stitches. Work as above, increasing to 11 stitches in 2nd round. Work 22 rounds, BUT on the 21st round, increase 2 stitches (one at each side). Hook up ladders. Put all 14 stitches on a thread.

I-Cord Index Finger: *(make 2)* Cast On 6 stitches. Work as above, increasing to 11 stitches in 2nd round. Work 20 rounds. Hook up ladders. Put all 12 stitches on a thread.

I-Cord Thumb: *(make 2)* Cast On 6 stitches. Work as above increasing to 11 stitches. Work 16 rounds. Hook up ladders. Put all 12 stitches on a thread.

Assembly: on 4 d.p. needles, pick up 10 stitches from Index, 5 from one side of Middle, 9 from around Ring, 5 from other side of Middle. This leaves 2 opposed pairs of raw stitches between the 3 fingers. Work

around on these 29 stitches for 2 rounds. Add in the Pinky (8 stitches) for a total of 37 stitches - again leaving 2 opposed pair of raw stitches on threads. Knit around for 2½", or wanted depth to thumb crotch.

Decide on Palm or Side thumb placement, and remember to mirror-image the other hand. Put 3 hand stitches (centered on the side stitch - OR just inside the side stitch for a "palm" thumb), match 3 thumb stitches and knit around rest of 9 thumb stitches (total 43 stitches). Knit one round.

Thumb Gusset #1: *(photo opposite, left)* At thumb corner, SSK, K 7 thumb stitches, K2 tog. K 2 rounds plain. Repeat decrease - with only 5 stitches between this time. Continue decreasing every 3rd round until only 1 stitch separates the decrease lines. Work a final Double-Decrease of Slip 2 tog K'wise, K1, pass 2 slipped stitches over.

Thumb Gusset #2: *(photo opposite, right)* *K to within center 5 thumb-stitches: K2 tog, K1, SSK. K 2 rounds plain. Repeat from * three more times, keeping the decreases in a vertical line.

Try the glove on. Have you reached the wrist? If not, work the necessary additional rounds to do so.

Wrist Shaping: (K6, K2 tog) 4 times, ending K1 (29 stitches). Work plain for 1". Increase to 40

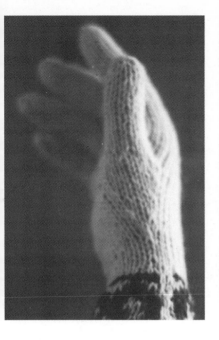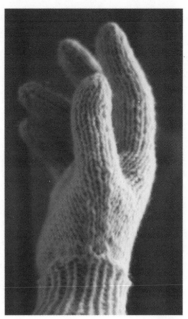

stitches by alternating K3, M(ake) 1, and K2, M1;
ending K1.

Gauntlet: Establish pattern *(see p59)*, dividing the
number of stitches at the sides, and knitting one pattern
repeat on the front and one on the back. Mark the 3
un-pattern stitches (#1, 19 and 20 on the chart) at each
side of the gauntlet, and keep them in light, dark, light.
This makes a nice stripe up the sides - like a Norwegian
mitten - and prevents a long carry. Follow the 4 pairs of
increases as indicated on the chart. You may switch to an
11½" circular needle if you like.This gauntlet is a great
place to experiment with patterns, textures and shapes;
we have a slew of ideas for our next pair.

I-Cord Casting Off: Cast On 3 stitches by making
3 backward loops over the R needle. Transfer the 3
stitches to L needle and *K2, slip 1 (Cord st), K1 (raw st),
psso. Replace 3 stitches to L needle and repeat from * all
around top of cuff. Weave end to beginning.

Weave fingers to prevent holes, pick up an extra "stitch" each side of the 2 stitches on threads. You will be weaving 4 stitches to 4 between each finger, and 5 to 5 for thumb crotch. Darn in all ends.

Bonus Hat: (We actually knitted the hat first to check our gauge, and to experiment working with two different weights of wool; the dark is heavier than the light. When you find yourself in this situation, use the heavier wool for the color pattern, as it will stand out nicely. In reverse, the pattern is liable to sink into the background.) Cast On 84 stitches. Work ribbing for an inch or so, and increase to 108 in next round (K4, M1, cheating three times to end up with 108). You will be able to fit in 6 full repeats of this 18-stitch chart. The top is shaped by a double-decrease worked 9 times every 3rd round. We knitted vertical striped leading up from the final crosses at the top of the chart. Every third stripe becomes a double-decrease point, which gradually consumes the other stripes. Pom-pom optional.

hat chart

Chart

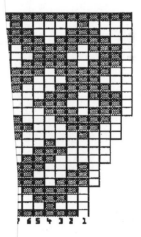

CHAPTER SIX

Shawl Collared Vest

March '93. Dear Knitter,

Lace knitting and Sock knitting seem an incongruous pair, yet many of you needn't be told that both are riding a wave of popularity at present. Knitting your own stockings is not practical; it is not economical - so what is the appeal? There seems to be a deeply embedded, yet indefinable memory calling multitudes of knitters to become engrossed in this most ancient form of our most ancient craft; a link with the original knitters. And, when presented with a pair of handknitted stockings, the recipient is nearly always rhapsodic; perhaps they feel a flicker of the historical link as well. Look up Pablo Neruda's poem, *Ode To My Socks*.

Be all this as it may ... socks are *not* the topic of this chapter.

SHAWL-COLLARED VEST - general notes

We have combined three most often requested garments: a shawl collar, a V-neck cardigan and a vest.

For minimal decoration, we chose a simple 3 over 3 cable *(p68. 69)* and once we got going, realized how long it had been since we last knitted this appealing design. As knitters increase their skills, they naturally want to increase the challenges in their knitting, and tackle ever more difficult cables. To step back to this classic twist is refreshing and caused us to see anew the beauty in its simplicity.

The shawl collar aspect of the design suggested to us a moderately heavy wool, and we picked our 3-ply natural Sheepswool; the same wool we used for the *Puzzle-Pillow Blanket* in Chapter One. A swatch showed that we preferred 3¼ stitches to 1" for this project (although we liked the look and feel of 3½ stitches to 1" as well ... Knitter's Choice), so we plugged that gauge into EPS to get our working numbers. We will make the garment slightly oversized as we have an image of an Outdoor Person wearing this vest over another sweater.

The vest is worked in the round from the lower

edge. Begin with ribbing, into which we inserted the cables and steek stitches. Increase to 100% [K] above the ribbing, and continue to wanted length to underarms (allowing for a nice deep armhole), adding 2 sets of spaced increases at the sides to counteract the "taking in" of the cables. Put 3-4" worth of stitches on a thread, and cast on 5 steek stitches in their place for the armholes.

Begin the V-Neck shaping at the same time by decreasing outside the center cables every 3rd or 4th round - depending upon the wanted angle of the V. When about 6½-7" worth of stitches have been consumed by the shaping, continue straight to wanted shoulder height. Machine stitch and cut the armholes and center front. The armhole borders and shoulder seams can be worked in one unbroken flow. Finally, knit up stitches from fronts and neck and knit the shawl collar. Embellish it with I-Cord Tab Buttonholes .

We are quite pleased with our current technique for finishing a cut edge. We don't mind herringbone stitch neatening for armholes, but we are much fussier when it comes to cardigans. Armhole edges are really only seen by the wearer, but cardigan edges are liable to flap open and no matter how neatly you've cross-stitched over the cut edge, it looks a bit untidy. We have come up with an alternative method which combines both the Norwegian and Scottish methods; see ahead for instructions.

SHAWL COLLARED VEST
specific directions

SIZE: chest circumference 40 (44, 48)". Suggested length 25 (27, 28½)".

GAUGE: 3¼ stitches to 1". 13 stitches to 4".

MATERIALS: 5 (6, 7) 4oz skeins of 3-ply Sheepswool (in natural Cream, Pale Grey, Medium Grey or Blacksheep). A 16", 24" and 40" circular needle of a size to give you the above gauge (approximately #6-8). A smaller size 24" for the ribbing (optional). 3 buttons.

Using **EPS** *(Elizabeth's Percentage System)*, the Key Number [K] is obtained by multiplying gauge times wanted circumference at the widest point: 130 (144, 156). To hold in the lower ribbing, cast on about 10% fewer stitches and take a smaller size needle if wanted. 5 "steek" stitches are added at center front to provide a field for the future machine-stitching and cutting. They are not part of the measurement. ("Steek" is a Scottish colloquialism for the extra sts.)

Cast On 116+5 (132+5, 140+5) stitches. Work in K1b, P1 rib and establish the 4 cable sections as follows: 2 at centers F(ront) and B(ack) (see drawing), allowing a single Knit Up Stitch each side of the 5 steek stitches for picking up the border later. A Cable Section = P1, K1b,

P1, 6-st cable, P1, K1b, P1. (see photo). Work 5-6 rounds before crossing the first cable, inserting a set of short rows across the back in the ribbing to counteract the dreaded riding-up (we forgot to do this). Knit ribbing to

wanted depth (about 3-4"). Increase to [K] by adding 14 (12, 16) stitches to the first round above the ribbing; sneakily hiding 8 of the increases each side of each cable in the purl sections - altering the Cable Section to P1, K1b, P2, cable, P2, K1b, P1. Add the other 6 (4, 8) increases more or less evenly spaced in the side sections.

Mark the side "seam" stitches. Work the cables every 8th round. Knit to wanted length to underarm; approximately 14 (15, 16)" ... increasing 2 stitches each side at the 9" point and again at 12" from lower edge as follows: K to 1 stitch before marker, M1, K3, M1. Repeat at other side.

The number of stitches to put on a thread at the underarms will determine the final shoulder width, so add more if want a narrow shoulder, or fewer for wider shoulders. We put 11 (13, 15) stitches on threads at each underarm, centered directly above the marked stitches. Cast on 5 steek sts in their place and continue.

At the Same Time (as they say), work V-Neck Shaping every 3rd round as follows: *Knit across R front cable section, SSK. Work around back to within 2 stitches of L front cable section, K2 tog. Work 2 rounds straight. Repeat from * 6 times more; then change the rate to every 4th round 5 times. Now work straight to wanted armhole depth 11" (12, 12½)"

Put all sts on a thread. Baste down centers of all steeks. Put on your good glasses, and machine-stitch (with small stitch and loose tension) down R and up L side of the very center stitch. Cut carefully between the machine-stitching.

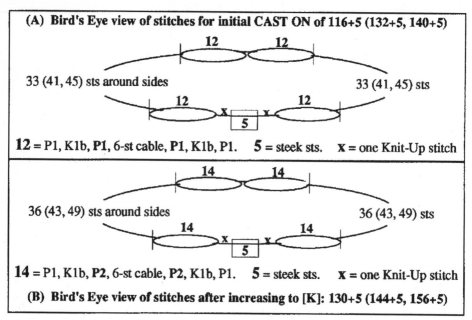

(A) Bird's Eye view of stitches for initial CAST ON of 116+5 (132+5, 140+5)

12   12

33 (41, 45) sts around sides   33 (41, 45) sts

12   12

x   x
5

12 = P1, K1b, P1, 6-st cable, P1, K1b, P1.   **5** = steek sts.   **x** = one Knit-Up stitch

14   14

36 (43, 49) sts around sides   36 (43, 49) sts

14   14

x   x
5

14 = P1, K1b, P2, 6-st cable, P2, K1b, P1.   **5** = steek sts.   **x** = one Knit-Up stitch

(B) Bird's Eye view of stitches after increasing to [K]: 130+5 (144+5, 156+5)

Armhole Border: beginning at shoulder on 3rd stitch from cut edge, knit up 2 stitches for every 3 rounds down 1 side. knit all underarm "holding" stitches (twisting a loose thread at each corner, and knitting it as a stitch). and 2 for 3 up the other side. Work back and forth for 2 ridges of garter-stitch. Do not break wool.

Elizabeth's I-Cord Casting Off At shoulder top, Cast On two I-Cord stitches. Transfer them to L needle and *K1, K2 tog tbl (through-back-loop) - being the last Cord stitch and 1 "raw" stitch. Replace to L needle, and repeat from * around armhole stitches, plus a strand from the I-Cord Cast On, uniting the armhole. Do not break the wool, but continue to join the shoulder seams:

Meg's 3-Needle I-Cord Cast Off: first place F and B shoulder stitches on 2 needles (including 2 stitches from each just-completed armhole border). The 2 armhole I-Cord stitches are on the 3rd needle. Place them onto the back shoulder needle. *K1, Slip 1, K2 tog (being 1 each from F and B needles), psso. Replace to B needle.

Repeat from * across shoulder. Put the 2 Cord stitches on a thread. Repeat on other side.

Shawl Collar: from lower L front corner - into the

"knit-up stitch" - knit up 2 stitches for every 3 rounds up to shoulder. Knit the 2 waiting Cord stitches; every stitch across the neck back (from holder); 2 more Cord stitches and 2 for 3 down R side. There is usually a looseness at each neck corner ... pick up the loose strand, twist it, put it on he needle and call it a stitch - as you did at armhole corners. Turn. Slip 1 P'wise on all first stitches throughout the collar; we will say "K20", but we mean "Slip 1 P'wise, K19". K to 10 stitches past the center neck-back. Turn, K20. Turn, K22. Turn, K24. turn, K26, etc. After 8 ridges, mark the collar stitch that leads to each shoulder seam (about 24 stitches apart) and Increase between the marked stitches across the back collar as follows: M1, (K3, M1) 7 times, M1. Now, begin to nibble up 3 stitches at the end of each short

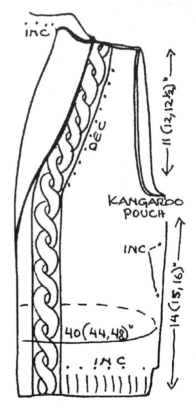

row instead of 2. Continue back and forth until you reach the beginning of the V-neck shaping (about 16 ridges at neck-back).

Work back and forth on all border stitches for 4 more rows (2 ridges) - or more if you'd like a wider edging. Cast off in 2-stitch I-Cord Cast Off as you did on the armholes; adjusting for tension.

Elizabeth's I-Cord Tab Buttonholes: mark 3 button locations. With smaller d.p. needle, knit up 6 stitches into the 2nd border ridge from the body. Work back and forth for 2 or 3 ridges. Now, on first 3 stitches only: K2 tog, K1. Replace to L needle. *K2, replace. Repeat from * until the I-Cord makes a loop size to accommodate your chosen buttons (about 8-9 rounds). On the last rowlet of I-Cord, increase back up to 3 stitches and weave to the 3 waiting stitches. Secure tab to garment as you darn in the ends. Sew on buttons.

Finishing Cut Edges: if you stitched into the L and R halves of the very center steek stitch, you will now simply fold the 2½-stitch flap to the inside. With regular (matching) sewing thread and needle, tuck under **only** the half stitch with the machine-stitching in it, and tack the edge down. Weave the 2 raw steek stitches to each other at the shoulder top. Result: a smooth 2-stitch wide facing, and, because the half-stitch you tucked underneath was machined first, it was also flattened for minimal bulk. Neat, huh?

ADDITIONAL NOTES

To turn a 3/3 cable *with a spare* needle for **R over L Cable**: slip first 3 stitches onto spare needle and hold in *front* of work. K last 3 stitches, then K 3 from spare needle. For **L over R Cable**: slip first 3 stitches onto spare needle and hold in **back** of work. K last 3 stitches, then K 3 from spare needle.

To turn a 3/3 cable *without a spare needle* you need to change the position of the stitches on the L needle. **R over L Cable**: slip next 6 stitches off the needle. Pick up the first 3 stitches with L needle in front of work. Pick up the last 3 with R needle behind, and transfer them to L needle. Now, K 6. **L over R Cable**: slide next 6 stitches off L needle. Pick up first 3 with L needle in back. Pick up last 3 with R needle in front, and slip them onto L needle. K 6.

The **Reversible Phoney Seam on Shawl Collar** is worked as you are casting off. Find the stitch that leads from the shoulder seam to the top of the collar. Drop it off the needle, and cause it to run down to the beginning of the collar. Separate the ladders into Front and Back. With a crochet hook, grab the bottom stitch and hook up all the Front ladders (actually, every other one). Put it on the needle. Turn the collar over, find a strand at the base of the collar; twist it and call it a stitch. Now hook up all the Back ladders (actually other every one). As you cast off those 2 stitches, knit them together as one.

If you find a largish hole at the bottom corner of the armhole (as we did - in spite of the twisted strand), work a duplicate stitch over it.

That's it. We spliced in each new skein as described on pages 9-10, so had minimal ends to darn in.

Meg (wearing the new vest) and the cat, Carl.

CHAPTER SEVEN

Round-the-Bend Jacket

September, 1990. Dear Knitter,

Advance warning: we did not name this design *Round-The Bend* for nothing ... it nearly drove us there. With that disclaimer in mind please join us if you're game; perhaps comforted by testimonials on file from many knitters who have completed this design with great success, and were intrigued by the challenge.

The jacket is knitted in two halves - with a proper vent at center back - but is No-Sew throughout. The sleeves are stocking stitch, the body is garter-stitch. There is something going on every minute and it is a rather unique method of construction.

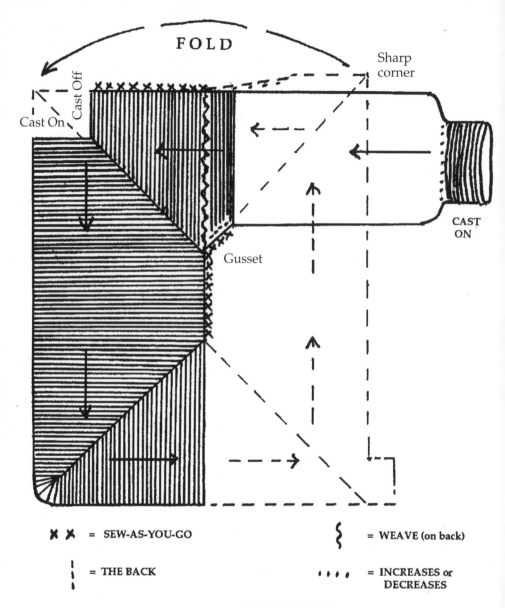

FOLD

Sharp corner

Cast On

Cast Off

Cast On

CAST ON

Gusset

✗ ✗ = SEW-AS-YOU-GO

⌇ = WEAVE (on back)

⋮ = THE BACK

♦ ♦ ♦ ♦ = INCREASES or DECREASES

EXPOSITION
(detailed instructions follow)

Left Half: Cast On at the cuff and work in garter-stitch to wanted depth. Double the number of stitches, join and continue around in stocking stitch. Follow the drawing, and work to 2½" shy of wanted length to underarm (erring on the too-long side to allow the bloused sleeve to blouse). Switch back to garter-stitch and work the Gusset.

Abandon the back half of the sleeve stitches, and turn the first corner on the front half of the stitches. At 3" from corner point, Cast Off 3" worth of stitches, and Cast On 4" worth of stitches. Complete corner.

Work straight until piece measures a front-panel-width *less* than wanted total length. i.e. if your jacket is 22" wide, the front panel is 11" across. When you are 11" shy of wanted total length, turn the 2nd corner - making a rounded point if wanted.

Turn 3rd corner, adding vent flap.

As you work the straight bit up the back, unite it to the front selvedge at the same time.

Turn 4th corner down to a sharp point. As you turn it up again and have passed the 4" mark, fold the piece - wrong sides together - and unite the shoulders as you finish turning the corner ... remembering to decrease the 4 stitches you added at the neck-front. When the corner has been turned, you will find yourself at the abandoned stitches of the back of the sleeve. Weave them to the end of the 4th corner.

Make the **Right Half**, working mirror-imaging on corners, and reversing the Sew-As-You-Go technique *(see ahead)*. (Do not make another vent flap).

The center back will be knitted together and Applied I-Cord added to the entire perifery incorporating the looped buttonholes as you go. The cuffs will be bordered by I-Cord, and their seams united by 3-Needle Cast Off. Tack down the inside of the vent flap. Sew on buttons (aha! there *is* some sewing in this thing), and call a psychiatrist: you've gone 'round the bend!

ROUND-THE-BEND - specifics

SIZE: 44" chest circumference

GAUGE: 4 stitches to 1"

MATERIALS: seven 4oz skeins Lovat, two skeins Teal (or Sorrel) *Highland Wool* from Scotland (the very wool used to weave Harris Tweed; nice and hairy and tough). A tad of 3-ply pale Grey *Sheepswool;* enough for 3 ridges. A 16" and 24" circular needle of a size to give you wanted gauge; approximately #6-9. A set of 6 porcelain Iris Buttons in Blue or Rust. d.p. needles for I-Cord trim. The above are the colors of the prototype. Naturally you may choose from other colors *(like Plum & Burgundy, Plum & Bressay Blue, Acorn and Sorrel)* or other wools.

Instructions for size 44" follow. Use the percentages given to alter to your size and gauge. Study the schematic to see where you are and where you're going.

This jacket is knitted in two halves with sleeves in stocking-stitch; body in garter-stitch. Because of the beautiful squareness of garter-stitch, it is ideal for figuring size and measurement: 2 rows = 1 ridge. 5 stitches and 5 ridges = a perfect square, as will any number of stitches and an equal number of ridges.

Determine how wide you want your jacket to be, multiply that by your gauge; take half of that for each quarter.

Even if you already know how to turn a corner in garter-stitch, we recommend that you make a swatch - not only obtain your gauge, but alto to decide whether you want Holes or No Holes, and a selvedge of slip K'wise or slip P'wise.

To demonstrate all four possibilities, knit the following ....

SWATCH: Cast On 15 stitches *(we also slip all first selvedge stitches)*

K14, turn, slip 1 K'wise, K to end.

K13, turn, slip 1 K'wise, K to end.

K12, turn, slip 1 K'wise, K to end.

K11, turn, slip 1 K'wise, K to end.

K10, turn, slip 1 K'wise, K to end.

K9, turn, slip 1 K'wise, K to end.

K7, Wrap *(slip next stitch, wool forward, replace stitch; see p35)*, turn, K to end.

K6, Wrap, turn, K to end.

K5, Wrap, turn, K to end.

K4, Wrap, turn, K to end.

K3, Wrap, turn, K to end.

K2, Wrap, turn, K to end. Now turn the corner back up again as follows:

K2, K wrap & slipped stitch tog, turn, slip 1 K'wise, K back.

K3, K wrap & slipped stitch tog, turn, slip 1 K'wise, K back.

K4, K wrap & slipped stitch tog, turn, slip 1 K'wise, K back.

K5, K wrap & slipped stitch tog, turn, slip 1 K'wise, K back.

K6, K wrap & slipped stitch tog, turn, slip 1 K'wise, K back.

K7, K wrap & slipped stitch tog (8th stitch), turn, slip 1 K'wise, K back.

K9, turn, slip 1 K'wise, K back.

K10, turn, slip 1 K'wise, K back.

K11, turn, slip 1 K'wise, K back.

K12, turn, slip 1 K'wise, K back.

K13, turn, slip 1 K'wise, K back.

K14, turn, slip 1 K'wise, K back.   K15.

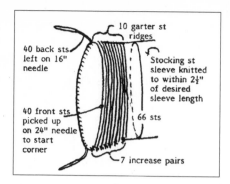

40 back sts left on 16" needle

10 garter st ridges

Stocking st sleeve knitted to within 2¼" of desired sleeve length

40 front sts picked up on 24" needle to start corner

66 sts

7 increase pairs

Take a look at your finished swatch and decide which of the four pleases you most. (We chose wraps and slipped-stitches P'wise.)

4 stitches to 1" x 44" around = 176 or Key Number [K], or 44 stitches per quarter. Adjust these numbers to your wanted circumference and gauge.

Left Section, Cuff: with 16" circular needle, **Cast On** 33 (19% of [K]). Work back and forth in garter-stitch for 11 ridges (22 rows). Double the number to 66 (38% of [K]) by working K1, M1 across all stitches, for a blousy sleeve.

Sleeve: join the cuff edge into a circle, and switch to stocking stitch. (For a tapered sleeve, you may want to cast on a few more stitches for the cuff, and increase 2 stitches every 5th round.) At 2½" shy of wanted sleeve length to underarm, begin to work back and forth in garter-stitch, changing color for stripes: 1st ridge in pale grey, then 9 ridges in stripe color. At The Same Time, work a **gusset** as follows: increase 2 stitches at underarm every 2nd ridge 3 times, then every ridge 4 times (14 new stitches).

During this garter-stitch burst, you may **"Sew"As You Go**: work to the last stitch, Wrap the next stitch (which will be the first stitch of that row), turn, repeat from *. After the gusset increase you will have 80 stitches (45% of [K])

First Corner: abandon the back half of the sleeve stitches (40 stitches for us) by leaving them on the 16" needle. Switch to a 24" length needle for the first corner.

Beginning at sleeve top,

K40, turn, K back.

K39, turn, K back.

K38, turn, K back.

K37, turn, K back.

K36, turn, K back, etc (remembering to work Wrapping at each turn if you selected the No-Holes version).

When 12 stitches (3" worth) remain on the corner, **cast them off**. Now **cast on 16** stitches (4" worth) to achieve the 11" wide right front (44" around), without have a too-voluminous sleeve.

Complete corner, add stripes to match sleeve, and work straight until you are 11" shy of wanted total length.

Turn 2nd corner in the same direction, and shape a **Rounded Corner** by not working all the way down to the last two stitches as follows: work down to K5, turn, K back. Now K6, turn, K back. K7, etc, back up to K44. Immediately begin to **turn 3rd corner**.

Jacket Vent (on L half only): when you are down to K2, turn, K back, add the vent by **casting on 8 stitches**. Turn the corner up again, and, at 20 ridges from lower edge, **cast off the 8 vent stitches**. Complete the corner.

Work the back straight up, and **"Sew" As You Go** by picking up (on a d.p. needle) 1 stitch for each ridge along the selvedge of the completed front. On "right" side of work *K **to within last stitch, SSK** (being last stitch on needle plus one picked-up selvedge stitch), **turn, wool forward, slip 1st stitch**

P'wise. Repeat from * on every "right" side. This produces a super-neat seam consisting of a single vertical

stocking-stitch *(photo on p77)*. Don't forget to work the matching stripes.

Turn 4th corner down to 2 stitches. As you turn back up again and get to K 16, fold the jacket in half (wrong sides together) and begin to unite the shoulders by a slight variation of "Sew" As You Go. This time you will be meeting the seam on the "wrong" side of he work: ***K to within last stitch, wool forward, slip 2 p"wise** (being the last stitch on the needle, plus one picked up shoulder selvedge stitch), **turn, K2 tog.** Repeat from * on every "wrong" side for the rest of the shoulder seam. *Stay alert on the second half of the jacket ... the No Sew moves will be reversed for the side- and shoulder-seams.*

The 4 extra stitches you added at the neck front (remember when you cast off 12, but cast on 16?) will now be decreased (by SSK or K2 tog) evenly-spaced over the remaining ridges.

When you have completed the final corner, weave the 40 stitches to the patiently-waiting stitches you abandoned on the 16" sleeve needle. Darn in all ends.

Knit second half **being careful to make a mirror image**: L side corners all turn L; R side corners all turn R. The appearance of the corners on L and R halves (whether holes or no-holes) will not match each other perfectly. We do not let this bother us, but take it as a fact of knitting. The maneuvers necessary to prevent this seem a bit masochistic in the face of what we are already going through.

I-Cord Finishing: this will complete the No-Sew

aspect of the jacket design. Line up the two halves ... center back selvedge bumped against center back selvedge. Using one d.p. needle for each selvedge, beginning at top of the vent - heading for the shoulders -

pick up about 10-15 stitches along each selvedge (1 stitch for each ridge). Now. Meg's **3-Needle I-Cord Cast Off** *(see p82)* was proposed to unite the back. The videographer (Camera Guy) was bothered about the wearer having to lean back on a thickish I-Cord running up the vertebrae. Lo and Behold, he "unvented" a variation right on the spot ... he's been taping too many knitting videos and knows more about the subject than he wants to. *(photo of the seam; top p77)*.

Cameraman's Variation: Cast on 3 I-Cord stitches in stripe color, and transfer them to *front* pick-up needle. ***K1, SSK** (being the 2nd Cord stitch plus first picked-up stitch on back needle), **K2 tog** (being 3rd Cord stitch plus first picked-up stitch on front needle), **replace 3 stitches onto front pick-up needle, and repeat from ***. How about that? A nice, flat, comfortable union of the two halves. Whatta guy. At the top of the seam, leave the 3 Cord stitches on a thread to be finished with the *Applied I-Cord* to come.

Applied I-Cord Around Entire Perifery: the Cord begins at top of vent flap, and works down the edge, across bottom of jacket, up one side, around neck, down other side, across bottom, and up to top of flap where you began. With smaller d.p. needle, pick up 1 stitch for each ridge on all vertical edges, and 1 stitch for each stitch horizontally. Pick up about 15-20 stitches at a time,

I-Cord them, then pick up some more. Onto regular-size needle, **Cast On 3** stitches. Transfer them to pick-up needle and *K2, **slip 1**(last Cord stitch), **K1** (picked-up stitch), **psso. Replace the 3 stitches to L needle**, and repeat from * around all edges. Decide whether you want buttonholes on the L or R front, then decide what type of buttonholes you want: **Hidden I-Cord**? *(At buttonhole site, work 3 rounds of I-Cord without attaching it to the selvedge; then slip 3 corresponding picked-up stitches off the d.p. needle, and begin attaching again as usual.)*. Or: **Loop I-Cord**? *(At buttonhole site, work the 3 Cord stitches for about 8 - 10 rounds ... as long as you need to accommodate the buttons you have chosen ... then begin attaching again - without skipping any picked-up stitches.)* We used an elongated Loop, but, as our buttons are rather small, we reduced the Cord from 3 to 2 stitches for the 35-40 rounds of Cord; then increased back up to 3 stitches to continue applying. Form the large loop into a figure eight, and

tack half of it down. Continue around and weave end to beginning. Sew on buttons.

I-Cord Cuff: finish this in one continuous stream: work Applied I-Cord around lower edge; work 3-Needle I-Cord Cast Off to unite the selvedges, then Applied I-Cord around the last garter-stitch ridge to hold the cuff snugly; this is what causes the sleeve fabric to gather so nicely. *(see photo)* Weave end to beginning.

Vertical After-Thought Pocket: we plan to add pockets one of these days ... in the vertical section near the side "seam", snip a stitch in the middle of the wanted pocket opening. Ravel stitches in both directions to wanted width. Cast off the front raw stitches in 2-stitch

I-Cord. Pick up the back raw stitches, and work back and forth for pocket (in stocking-stitch with garter-stitch edges for non curling), using, perhaps, matching Shetland wool for less bulk. Gradually decrease at the top edge as you head for the corner. Tack down the edges.

Some *Round-the-Bend* Techniques

[A] M(ake) 1 - make a backward loop (half hitch) over the right-hand needle.

A

[B] KNITTED-ON CASTING ON - To add stitches in the middle of a garment, knit into the first stitch on the L needle. Put the new stitch onto the L needle. Now: * insert R needle between 1st and 2nd stitch on L needle, draw working wool through and place the loop on L needle. Repeat from *.

[C] SSK - slip 2 stitches separately, knitwise. Put the tip of the L needle into them from left to right; knit them together. *(Experiment with S 1 K, S 1 P, then K 2 tog.)*

C

[D] Basic FREE STANDING I-CORD (3 stitch)- Cast On 3 sts. *K3, replace onto L needle and repeat from * to wanted length.

[E] APPLIED I-CORD - on the "wrong" side, with a smaller d.p. needle, pick up one stitch for each ridge along the selvedge. On regular-size needle, Cast On 3 sts in border color. Transfer the 3 sts to the d.p. needle and *K2, slip 1, K1 (a picked-up stitch), psso. Replace the 3 sts to the

D

pick-up needle and repeat from *.

[F] 3-Needle I-Cord Cast Off - this will join two pieces of knitting and apply I-Cord at the same time.. Line up the raw sts of each piece on two needles and hold them parallel to each other. With the 3rd needle, Cast On 3 sts. Transfer to one of the other needles and *K2, slip 1, K2 tog (being 1 raw stitch from each needle), psso. Replace 3 sts to one of the L needles and repeat from *.

[G] Applied I-Cord Corners - for outer corner, work to corner stitch. Knit all 3 I-Cord sts without attaching them. Attach corner stitch; then work another un-attached round. Continue on. By inserting 2 extra rounds you have provided sufficient fabric to turn a nice sharp 90° corner. For an inner corner: apply I-Cord to within one stitch of corner and K2, slip 1, K2 tog, psso.

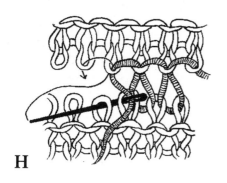

H

[H] WEAVING GARTER-STITCH Note that the **"ridge"** on the bottom is being woven to the **"valley"** at the top. The stitches must lie in this relationship to each other for a successful garter-stitch weave.

Needle Conversion Chart

American	British/Canadian	Metric (mm)
0000	17	1.25
000	16	1.50
00	15	1.75
0	14	2
1	13	2.25
		2.50
2	12	2.75
	11	3
3	10	3.25
4		3.50
5	9	3.75
6	8	4
7	7	4.50
8	6	5
9	5	5.50
10	4	6
10½	3	6.50
	2	7
	1	7.50
11	0	8
13	00	9
15	000	10

This chart is merely a guide ... please be aware that it is a jungle out there when it comes to standardization of needle sizes: different brands will vary slightly from each other in diameter. To this anomaly add the irregularities in the international comparisons and you will realize that you must trust your resulting GAUGE over the "size" written on the needle package.

Bibliography

Abbey, Barbara. *Barbara Abbey's Knitting Lace*. Pittsville, WI.
Schoolhouse Press, 1993

Johansson, Britta and Nilsson, Kersti. *Binge - en halländsk
stricktradition*. Stockholm, Sweden. LTs förlag, 1980

Kinzel, Marianne. *First Book of Modern Lace Knitting*. New York City,
NY. Dover Publications, Inc, 1972

_____. *Second Book of Modern Lace Knitting*. New York City,
NY. Dover Publications, Inc, 1972

McGregor, Sheila. *The Complete Book of Traditional Scandinavian
Knitting*. New York City, NY. St. Martin's Press, 1984

Royce, Beverly. *Notes on Double Knitting*. Pittsville, WI. Schoolhouse
Press, 1994

Zimmermann, Elizabeth. *Knitting Without Tears*. New York City,
NY. Charles Scribner's Sons, 1971

_____. *Knitter's Almanac*. New York City, NY. Dover
Publications, Inc, 1974

_____. *Knitting Workshop*. Pittsville, WI. Schoolhouse Press,
1981.

_____. *Knitting Around, or Knitting Without a License*.
Pittsville, WI. Schoolhouse Press, 1989.

Index

Supplies

As well as publishing knitting books and producing instructional knitting videos, *Schoolhouse Press* operates a mail-order business supplying knitters with a full range of tools and materials. All the wools, needles, buttons, etc used in the book/video, **Handknitting with Meg Swansen**, are available by mail.

Meg Swansen also teaches knitting at her annual summer Knitting Camp in central Wisconsin.

Schoolhouse Press, 6899 Cary Bluff, Pittsville, WI 54466.
telephone: (715) 884-2799.   fax: (715) 884-2829.